AN UNTOLD CLOSURE

A Tale of Love, Loss, and the Long Road to Healing

Chiranjeevi

#1

Two souls once meant to be, now lost in silence,
Pretending the past has faded while it still
Haunts.

I'm assuming she's moved on, well, she must be,
I have only deepened the wounds she carries.

We both carry doubts, afraid to face the truth,
Trapped in the shadows of what remains
unresolved.

She tells herself she's healed, but likes posts about
my favorite songs,
A reminder that the past is never truly gone.

Nothing has ever felt bluer than this,
So, I wonder why not one more try, may be
until one of us dies?

Your blood red lipstick is the first thing I set my eyes
on,
though your eyes are the last thing I think about
before I close mine each night.

I often wonder what makes it so captivating,
Is it the color, reminding me of Adriana from
Midnight in Paris,
or the way you wear it so effortlessly?

Neither. I think it's the subtle curve you draw
on the left side of your lips, just a flick of shyness.
I've never seen anything more alluring in my
entire life.

I've walked past the tree in my front yard
countless times,
Never pausing to wonder why its flowers fall
when it's still full of life.

I thought it was the nature of all living things
to let go while they still thrive.

Years passed, flowers fell, leaves withered,
and eventually, the tree died.

But what amazed me was how the earth refused
to let go of the roots,
even when it knew there was no point in
holding on.

Just like me, holding onto our memories,
refusing to let go,
afraid of watching you fall away from me if I
do so.

I remember the day you said,
"Now I know how the sea feels when the sun
vaporizes its water."

But, honey, little did you know,
I was only trying to tell you
that the sea always forms a cloud
to pour back all the water it once lost.

As you were recovering from your last
heartbreak,
I couldn't tell you about the Black Baccara rose
plant
I brought from my only garden.

"What if she thinks I'll just add more pages
to her lonely journal?" I thought.
So, I waited for the day you'd stop searching for
healing flowers in a graveyard.

But as days passed, you found funeral orchids
and mistook them for roses, again.

I promise you this, I'll keep watering my plant
every day, growing more roses until you find
your way to my garden.
So, you can heal, and in your presence,
I'll heal myself, eventually.

Just when I thought I was sailing in the
ocean of happiness, a storm of melancholy
hit me and destroyed my boat, which I named
Hope.

But I'll tell you this, Nature may be unkind to
me now,
I might be swimming in a shoreless sea of gloom,
but it will only persist until I swim across
to reach the shores of Perseverance Island.

There, I'll find myself a new boat,
and I'll name it *Hope* again.

As far back as I can remember,
people who promised they would stay till the
end
have become the songs I skip in my playlist
but never delete.

June 2013,

Under the never-ending sky, you came into my life like a falling star.

Dreams felt real only because you were beside me.
God! It was magical back then.

I would've never survived those days if you weren't a firework
lighting up my lonely, dark nights.

A conversation with you felt like reading
an unpublished fantasy book called *Abyss of Love*.
In the preface, you spoke of your admiration for galaxies,
hills, and your white painted room,
which you filled with little yellow lights.

Certain books can never be understood by everyone,
but to me, you are as familiar as my first home.
So, if I don't turn a page every day,
it would feel like standing on an abandoned beach,
without tides, without breeze.

What a waste of hope,
only to find constant blank pages
right after my favorite chapter,
titled *Annihilation of Soul*.

#10

Collection of Haiku:

On a rainy night,
when coffee and showers failed,
your thoughts warmed my soul.

Your silence, when I
need you loud, is heard by all
in my world, through me.

I still chose to cross
skies for you, knowing you'd
greet me with goodbye.

Recurring thoughts of
past, unknown stories of fate,
in between myself.

#11

Felt my broken heart
getting back to its shape with
your subtle touch.

A rotten flower
shouldn't expect bees to come
bloom, and they will find.

You and I, a grave
Buried soul's sacred song over
unsettling holler.

Cinquin:

Your laugh
a tune rhymed to
my broken heart's holler
a melody with wings to heal
my doomed soul.

When our time comes,
we'll realize that life is but
an ocean full of memories.

Whether it's polluted or pure
depends on who and what
you invite to be a part of it.

Your goodbye texts weigh on my mind,
like the haunting lyrics of *Do I Wanna Know*.

When it ended, I wasn't searching for reasons,
just the unbearable thought of a life without you.

Yet you never truly left, not really,
you lingered in the moon's light, in the rain's
scent.

Every quiet night, every bite of orange fudge,
you were there, filling the emptiness I couldn't
escape.

I stopped listening to that song,
but someday, when memories fade, I'll play it
again to find you.

How heartbreaking it is to discover
that you were never a pearl in my island of
treachery,

but just a tiny rock,
shining only under the moonlight's beam.

I wish I had introduced you to the sun first.

On your deathbed, what do you wish to be
reminded of?
The final thought you'd carry with your soul?

The fragrance of milk, that's what I smelled
when my mom held me for the first time.

Her merry laugh was louder than my cry that
night,
and the touch of her lips on my forehead told me
all the pain was worth it for those nine months.

It must've been the coldest night of my life,
but the first sight of her filled me with warmth.

How I came into this world is how I wish to
leave,
all my senses should remind me of everything
my mom did for me.

Dark clouds and no stars,
Where do you take me tonight?

The frosty wind reminds me of her warmth,
But the drizzle drenches me in thoughts of her
absence.

This is the kind of night I would like to be
vulnerable,
Yet no night has passed without carrying you in
my heart and mind.

So, I hope you'll take me to the healing city,
Where broken hearts can mend.

#17

Out of all the nights that have passed,
The night we first came together,

The night that kept me awake with restless
thoughts of us,
The night I smelled your fragrance on my shirt,

That was the night I wished to dwell on forever,
But you made sure it lasted only until dawn.

A clap of despair struck me,
Leaving me forever sabotaged.

An empty heart yearning to be filled,
With the feeling of truly being alive.

Lately, I've been doubting my birth, life, and
death,
Will I ever feel beloved on this earth?

Or will this be just another regret
I carry to my deathbed?

#19

Dear November,
Your days are cold, and your nights are warm.
The flowers don't bloom, and you're a
melancholy storm.

Your dawns are terrifying, while dusks offer
comfort,
Yet why do I still hold you as my dearest month?

For it was you who brought us together,
And in this saudade life, I guess this is forever.

So far,
I have been the earth that cannot pursue rain,
Whenever the cloud pours in, I had to accept.

I have been the dark, wishing for light at night,
Only when the moon comes out, I can shine.

I have been the leaf that falls during autumn,
To blossom, I had to wait until it's spring.

But after all, as a human I am,
I wish I could at least get the love I need,
And not wait until it's too late.

#21

I wonder how do I exist in your memory?
When you hear someone calling my name?
When you listen to my favorite lines
From "Knee Socks"?

When the taste of your evening coffee
Reminded you of our first meet?
When the glimpse of an early autumn
Reminded you of our favorite days?

When the breeze of an ocean
Felt like my fragrance?
When a warm shower on a lonely night
Felt like my touch?

What did I remind you of?

I hope I reminded you that
I left pieces of myself in all your senses,
so that at least in your thoughts,
I would feel alive.

A fleeting glimpse of your shadow on the
neighbor's wall
Brought sunshine to my withered garden,

And, since then, I've been finding healing
flowers
Growing from my wild trees.

At the early dusk today, when the sky remained
blue,
I saw the moon casting her glow, preparing for
the dark.
But what made me pause, standstill, and stare?
What made this moment different from
yesterday?

In the vast sky, the moon stood alone,
Knowing the stars wouldn't join her for a while.
Yet, she chose to shine, undeterred.

And in that moment, I thought,
If only I had the courage like her,
I would have lit all her dark nights.

Abuse is not a cloudburst,
it doesn't pour and vanish with time.
It is a snowstorm, unyielding,
staying as long as the cold remains,
leaving a glacier in your heart.

So, shine, my love,
shine as bright as the sun.
Not just to be warm,
but to never turn cold.

Your wardrobe is an art gallery,
each piece a portrait of you.
Mostly red, black, and pink,
hardly any white.

In your favorite dress,
I see your anger,
your elegance,
your love,
all at once.

But never have I found hope,
not even once.

Yet, you remain
the most beautiful art
I have ever come across.

The Night I Lost My Dawn

I should have flown with the storm
that carried away my only home.
But I stayed,
only to find memories
frozen into a dark cloud,
raining endlessly.

Thunderclaps echo in my head,
forsaken dreams linger in my heart.
Yet, the world around me
refuses to share its sunshine.

#27

I often ask myself,

Why did I simply walk past you
when I should have greeted you
with a glittering moonflower,
knowing what you had been through?

That day, you looked like a man
drowning in a sea
that only pulls the euphoric in.

This feeling of inferiority blinds me,
just as the morning mist
hides the rays of sunshine.

I wish I were the boy
you once fell for in middle school,
or at least
that random guy you sat beside
in the exam hall.

Maybe then,
all this would have been a little easier.

Our shadows met for the first time,

Like two clouds dissolving into each other,
casting the brightest shade upon the city,
where golden lilies and lavender bloom.

I wondered
if we could heal a city just by crossing paths,
what magic would unfold
if our souls were to meet?

I'll leave that thought with you,
by saying
no star in the universe
could ever outshine
the shade our shadows cast that day.

You are a wildflower,

Your journey from bud to bloom
has carried more agony than it should.

The winter storms showed no mercy,
nor did the summer sun.

Now I see why you keep
only three flowers close.

But I wish I were the tallest bloom
in the garden you blossomed,
I could have guarded you
with all my will,
the same way you now guard your petals.

It's so depressing how you couldn't tell,
How much I've been feeling for you,
From the way I look at you,
From the words I write about you.
Even the warmth in my voice
Wasn't much of some help.

Last spring, I saw an elder
Picking flowers from her garden.
She sent some to a temple,
And the rest to a nearby graveyard.

It reminded me of myself,
And the guy you once fell for.

#31

You asked me to talk about my favorite winter.
I must have told you about the winter I met you.
Since winter comes after fall,
all the trees in my garden were bare,
no leaves, no flowers,
but you bloomed.
And I knew then,
you were the only flower
to bloom in my garden during December.

Ever since you fell,
I couldn't choose my favorite winter
out of all the twenty-four winters I've spent.
If someone asked me the same question now,
I'd probably tell them about my worst winter,
the one that came last year,
because that's when you came back,
only to leave again.

If you were a dusk,
your anger would have set
to welcome a calm night.

If you were autumn,
the bloomed fragments of you
would have fallen.

If you were the sky,
the stars of saudade
would have twinkled and burst.

But I'm so glad you chose to be the earth,
you hold your roots firm,
so your trees can dance
to the winds of abuses.

#33

When I felt your presence for the first time,
standing at the threshold,
I knew you would leave a void inside me—
a void that would last forever.

That void is an abyss,
one that cannot be filled by the seven seas or the
tallest hills.

But with the touch of your warm hands,
the fragrance of your clothes,
the taste of your scent,
and the sound of my name in your voice,

You could fill that void,
and silence the echoes from the part of my soul I
lost.

So, you're leaving again?
To the caves of solitude,
far away from your haven.
a small world brimming with comfort and
affection,
insults and abuse, wrath and sorrow.

You're ensuring no one follows,
neither to your refuge nor to your cave.
Afraid of what others might bring,
should they step across your threshold.

Fair, utterly fair.
But I couldn't help but seek a space,
ever since I saw the sadness behind your smile.

So, all I'm asking for is a place,
small enough for me to breathe in your world.
And I'll gather every star in the heavens,
to fill your nights with light and warmth.

And why would I do that?
Because you are worth every star,
for the beautiful soul that you are.

#35

Why couldn't I shine like a new pearl,
when I'm surrounded by the glittering moon
and the sparkling sun?
My days are spent
doubting if I even belong here.
Even the time and place I find myself in
aren't kind.

I should have seen this ride for what it is.
The art I experienced, the music I listened to
they've all exaggerated the lives here.

No matter how rare and bright we are,
some pearls just don't shine,
even under the brightest star.

It terrified me to realize I'm running out of
words to write about you.
They used to pour out when my heart grew
heavy from longing for you, but now they don't
flow.
How long can my heart yearn for you?
After all, I'm just a wretched man.

What scares me most is that we might part ways,
and you'll never truly know how deeply I've felt
for you.
I wish what I read in *The Alchemist* were true,
that if your heart desires something, the universe
conspires to bring it to you.
If it could empathize with my feelings, it
would've brought us together.

But that's okay.
My thoughts of leaving you might make sense,
and my heart may stop yearning,
but my soul will never let you go.

Why?
Because I don't believe anyone could love you
more than I love you.

And then there's Instagram,
constantly reminding me we don't follow each
other.
What a mess.

I must have thought about you
a million times today,
we had an endless conversation
about the things you remind me of.
a maroon-colored wildflower,
a warm blanket on a cold night,
and every single closed door.

And just like that, my life was full of light,
with my eyes closed.

#38

I'm happy you finally got your wings to fly high,
but it also breaks my heart to know you might
not return to me.
I heard some roses don't bloom during
Valentine's Day,
and I thought to myself,
I fell for you when it was already too late.

I remember walking with you on a lonely road
for the first time.
You pulled me to your side and said,
the roads are violently silent,
that I could hear my heart whispering your name
all along.

A few years later, and thousands of miles away
from home,
on the lonely streets of Chennai,
I found you in every corner,
whispering my name,
as I hollered to the pain of you not being here.

I don't ask for much,
except for space in your world to grow a garden.
Together, we'll plant lavenders for your mood
swings,
white roses for your hope when things aren't
going well,
golden wildflowers for the will to do what you
love,
and purple orchids for me to offer you every
morning.

I'll nurture this garden and let the flowers
blossom
with every single joy you cast in the rays of
shine.

But with the space that's left for me,
I can only bury the buds I gathered for you.

It's okay to let the rain ruin your forest,
Or the thunderbolt that burns down the woods.
Let the wild trees die, scare off all the birds,
Watch as the gods' most beautiful creatures
Run back to their caves.

Let everything fall to the ground,
And die as the sun sinks low.
Tear your heart apart and let it bleed,
Until it can bleed no more.
Spend the night inhaling the ashes
Of your lost love.

But when the sun rises the next morning,
It will rise to grow the wild trees again.
Sit among the wildflowers,
And find your heart healing,
To the fragrance of lilies and lavenders.

The days I held you in my hands
Were the very days I struggled with myself.

You would calm my doubts and hide my pain
Every time I inhaled your breath.
The tons of ashes I discarded
Danced to the tunes of my emotions.

But now, the tunes have stopped,
The doubts no longer arise.
The pain will be faced without your presence.
You've been a good friend,
But it's time I walk alone.

#43

When I learned about the days that stole your
light,
I was ready to offer you my star,
A star that glitters only for broken hearts.
My world may have turned dark,
And my moon might have lost its shine,
but my heart would have bloomed,
knowing that you held my light.

Ah, not a day goes by
Without cursing the time that brought us
together,
too late, too late.
I left some poems here for you
If you ever come across the brightest star in the
sky
or a wildflower by a lakeside,
I hope you'll think of me and my poems.

#44

I heard you're terrified that
I might come back for the love I gave you.
Well, all the love I poured into you is yours to
keep.
If I ever return, I might give more,
But I will never take again.

If we ever meet again,
If this universe ever brings us together, even for
a brief moment,
I want you to look at me the same way you did
the night we met,
just to understand how I felt, longing for you
without a trace of hope.

The days I spent yearning for you are now
imprisoned in a single moment,
Waiting for our eyes to meet, just so it can be set
free.

#46

How am I supposed to be okay with the words
"life goes on,"
When my universe defies every wish I make,
When the events I witness only widen the void
in my heart?
To keep a flower alive, it needs light every now
and then,
It's a sin to expect it to bloom while hiding it
from the sun.

Dear God, don't blame us for turning into devils,
We were never introduced to your kindness.

Somewhere between the time I lost seeking
more love,
And the love I lost while chasing more time,
I lost my true self to this voyage called life.
I can't afford to reach the end without the man
who dreamt of it all,
So I'm unsure whether I should bring down hell
or soar to heaven.

But if I'm seeking what matters most, that is
myself,
I won't quit.

#48

Pain, over time, is an abyss.
No beginning, no end.
You float on wings of melancholy,
Unaware of past, present, future.

Even when the way out is near,
You stay trapped in your mind.
Once sorrow's strings attach,
You become a puppet to your devil,
Wishing only for wounds and scars.

So, fight not to dwell,
My friend, fight not to dwell.

Some nights are arduous,
No matter how beautiful the day,
Agony lingers in the quiet of night.
I wonder why the calmest nights are sometimes
the most violent.

I remember walking down my corridor at 3 AM,
The sky sparkling with stars, no clouds,
And the moon so bright, its beam so soft,
I felt the mist surround me.
And then, I found myself lost in thoughts of you
again.

When I came back to my senses,
The mist had vanished,
I thought dawn was near,
but no, the clouds had come,
hiding all the stars,
Blocking the moon's gentle glow.

It's funny how nature teaches.
That night, it taught me,
My thoughts of us aren't stars anymore,

but clouds that veil the beauty in my sky.
But that's okay, I guess,
As long as I end up with the rain and rainbows,
It's all good.

At sixteen, I prayed to God to quicken my
world,
I craved for everything to unfold swiftly,
And vanish just as rapidly.
It came to pass, though,
Isn't it curious how God answers our fervent
wishes?

It felt like living an entire lifetime in each
fleeting moment,
But now, at twenty-four, I yearn for a slower
pace.
I can scarcely recall the memories made along
the way.
When I glance back, it seems I've always longed
to be discovered,
Unable to keep up with the relentless march of
time.

Isn't it strange how our desires shift?
What once consumed my every thought,
Now feels distant, unwanted.

Oh, how I wonder,
Where can we find a guidebook to navigate this
life?

In the end, I brought myself alone
To the shores of new beginnings.
The promises made to my future self,
To bring you along, have crumbled.
I've arrived where I'm meant to be,
But it doesn't feel like home, not yet.

The man who once longed for you hopelessly,
Is lost somewhere in the vast ocean,
still chasing stars, believing they guide him to
you.
If you ever find him, he's yours to keep,
But as for me, I'm letting this boat drift away.

Dear God,
When my time comes on the last sunset,
when only minutes left for the night to fall and
for my soul to return to you,

I wish to lay alone and think about all the days I
made my mum laugh.
The sound of her merry should ring throughout
this universe,
so that I could follow them and sleep at her feet
for one last time.

#53

If I hadn't found a piece of myself in you,
I would have written all these poems about you.
Thought we both were two lost souls,
Going to end up finding each other.

But you are a cloud that never fades,
And I'm a blossom stuck on the earth.
Lately, I've understood that you either help me
bloom or ruin with your rain,
And the flowers don't fly, and clouds don't fall,
so our souls aren't meant to be together.

I have finally made peace with myself,
After letting you go.
Since there's no place for both of us in your boat
to sail,
I need not hope for a voyage chasing horizons
together.

I must let you know that I'm going to carry the
days I spent longing for you,
For out of everything I have been so far,
I love the guy in me who fell for you the most.

So be it hell or heaven,
I promise I will meet you where you are already
mine.

#55

All I ask in return is not to mistake
My love as a mist that disappears over time.
I have always been the sun that brings dawn after
a long night,
So honestly, I have no qualms about you
throwing all the inattention to me.

And it doesn't irk me a bit about you finding
shade of comfort in others,
Cause I know you will seek for me
When you realize you need light and not shade
to bloom.

#56

You were worried
About being ordinary
in the eyes of people around you,
So I turned you into a poem,
and ever since then,
the stars have been begging the moon
to be ordinary.

How strange it is, to know that
I had to bury the kid I used to be
for the world, so unkind,
someone who chased rainbows
on every rainy day, hoping it was a doorway
to a paradise where the kids don't grow.

Not a single Sunday afternoon felt like forever
back then,
Because I knew the dusk would gather all the
kids
Around the neighborhood later,
the dawns were spent not to kill our souls for
survival
but to live life.

And now, every night, the time after the last
meal of the day,
I have been feeling this melancholic pain within,
knowing that I could never go back in time
to be that kid anymore.

The tides of voices in my head weren't kind
lately,
Day and night trying to sweep away the only
hope
Boat I have tied to the shores,
The journey to the other side of the sea is so
long,
And I'm fragile and terrified,

Maybe I've been staying on the coast for way too
long,
Not sure if I own the shore or am just another
prisoner,
But for all I know, once the journey begins,
there's no looking back,
I'll be welcomed on the other side by people
bowing down as I bring them what they have
been longing for,
Hope.

My world exists only as far as I could see,
Beyond that, there's a void, an abyss filled with
nonentity.
When the time calls for my name,
When I must leave myself here to get there,
I hope there will be silence as loud as the noise
this world carries.

#60

I remember being a leaf in my dream once,
Blown away by the storm,
far from my home, I fell on an alien land,
only to get caught by the wildfire and turn into
ashes.

And I remember being a storm too,
I helped the wildfire cause conflagration,
Abducted leaves from their homes and carried
them off
to somewhere they couldn't survive,
And turned them all into ashes.

I woke up and realized,
It's better to go through the pain than to cause it.

Since the world went quiet,
I started wailing to the walls in my room,
they trembled and shed their life to the voices
from my head,
When the time called for its rupture,
it turned into ashes and fell over the place.

From the ashes, I heard the walls whispering the
most profound phrase,
It said, "Sometimes death is not the end of life,
It's just the beginning of eternal freedom."

Fifty feet apart, a million things to be noticed in
between
us that evening,
Yet I found your eyes waiting to be rescued
from all the
chaos it has seen so far.

A question from an unknown voice within
raised, "How do
you know if she's the one?"
I told myself, when I laid my eyes on her for the
first time,
Despite the distance, I felt like I was already
carrying her
in my arms.

If just a sight of you could make me forget the
world
around, wouldn't my soul bloom by your touch?

I had written enough to resolve the mystery
you've been carrying in your eyes for the past
584 days.
Never thought we would end up exactly the way
we first met at the threshold,
but I have a different heart now.

December had always been cruel to me,
so I know it must be this month if we ever
parted our ways.
Hope the walls we shared while it lasted
would never fall as long as this world exists,
or at least until my time calls for my name.

Under the same moon where both of us exist,
I will keep writing about you,
hoping that one day I will hear you call my
name.

Holding on to the
candle that you are,
I wish not to
strike a match on you,
even if it means
losing the last sight of light.

I wish I had remembered
the fragrance you carried
the day we stood side by side for the first time.

I was trembling,
not from fear, but from the weight
of your scent wrapping around me.

My heart grew soft,
my knees turned weak.

A trace of rose water,
a whisper of strawberry lip gloss,
the kind of scent
that made me dream of us.

But I wish I had forgotten
the stains of your touch,
pressed like echoes into my palms.

I had to dig the deepest grave
this earth has ever known,

burying every feeling I had for you
with the same hands
that once prayed you'd be mine.

After we parted ways,
I bloomed into a melancholic interlude
in a song meant for joy.

I spent so many nights yearning for you
that I forgot the warmth of being loved,
like the grass beneath the angel oak,
forever reaching for the sun.

If only you knew how much you meant to me,
you would have let me carve your name
into my destiny,
not just into my heart.

If I ever decide to write a book in my 60s,

I would begin with the Memories of my mother,
naming that chapter *The Life of an Altruistic Woman.*

I would probably drain the ink reminiscing
about
one forgotten Sunday's dusk,
when all the children played, unaware
that we would never meet again.

Then comes the first girl I ever loved at ten,
her handwriting etched into my memory,
the fragrance she carried when we sat side by
side.

Maybe I'd write of my wife and our children,
the life I learned to share
when I once thought it belonged to me alone.

But the epilogue?
it will be only about you,
a woman lost in her own world,
yet the one who found the writer in me.

#68

I have mastered the art of escape,
slipping through the cracks of the life I was
meant to live.

The locked rooms of regret and misery
stood with open doors, waiting to swallow me
whole.

*"This is the only way home, and it isn't far from
here,"*
darkness whispered as I left my body behind.

Through the last flicker of light before the door
shut,
I looked back at a life that never answered my
prayers,

And I whispered back,
*"I don't wish for it to be long either… take me home
now."*

She carried a hint of mystery in her eyes,
a silence woven with secrets untold.

Was she afraid that a fleeting gaze
might unveil the whispers of her soul?
Or was her mystery so sacred
that she saved it for the one
willing to bring down the moon,
just so its light could touch
every shadow she's ever braved?

Perhaps the stars will align with answers.
Until then, I'll mend my garden
with healing lavenders,
grown from the tears that once fell
to greet her one more time,
or perhaps, for the last time.

#70

The moon assimilates the sun
to look as bewitching as it is,
and the beam of light it spreads across the earth
brings hope to broken hearts.

Those who stay up all night in the dark,
yearning for the one person
who could bring the dawn for them.

The universe has never seen
the moon and the sun collide into each other,
not once in history.

But if they could,
I hope they would cast the brightest and most
radiant light,
letting the world know that
if we love someone else more than we love
ourselves,
the darkness within us would disappear.

If I am the moon,
then she is my sun.

Now that you've turned into a nightmare,
I laugh at all the nights I spent dreaming of us.

I spill my heart onto the world through my
words,
just to remind myself
there are still tears left to dry.

How many more sleepless nights
do I have to pay for loving you?
How many more summers and winters
until I know the difference?

I've rusted beneath the weight of your rainfall of
thoughts,
but honey, if I had known
this is how love would leave me,
I'd do it all again.

Because you're everything I want to fall for.

#72

Respawned, as if I have the strength to endure
another heartbreak,
All the shadows I once dwelled in, all the
darkness I cloaked,
yet my eyes still sought a light, a light that
promises a brighter tomorrow.

Then she arrived, adorned in a lime-tinged
glow,
Like a lily that drank from the sun's warmth,
History taught me to avoid lilies and sunshine,
but what choice do I have now?

I yearn for nothing but her fragrance,
A scent that pulls my favorite memories from the
past.

Her eyes, knowing just whom to cast their sight
upon,
Secrets deeply hidden inside,
A one-way ticket to her soul's sanctuary.

And though I thought my heart long entombed,
Her angelic tone revived it,
Guiding it back home.
Now, my heart whispers her name, forevermore.

#73

I fell for her during the autumn, when roses
don't bloom.
So, I borrowed a shade of her lipstick and turned
my clouds to red,
So when it rains, it pours roses.

I thought, if this doesn't proclaim to the world
that she belongs to me,
What else will?

How many more roofs do I have to rebuild?
All the storms of heartaches and melancholy,
Disguised as people with happy faces,
tore them apart but never brought a single
rainbow to my sky.

Yet, I don't feel like I'm done.
I have seen the hope of sunshine through these
dark clouds,
So I'm keeping my shelter wide open this time.
May it come, be it a storm or a cloudburst,
I'll never quit until all the seven colors fill my
sky.

In my neighbor's garden, the flowers bloom as if they are being sent to heaven.
He tosses seeds like confetti on the soil, the earth cloaks them, and the rain nurtures the plants.

Elsewhere, I place them like a nurse places a newborn in her mother's hand.
We sow the seeds from the same plant, the sun shines and the rain fall on both of our gardens.

Yet, I reap the lifeless seeds out, and he plucks the flowers and sends them to a graveyard.
It's just a matter of blessing and curse, isn't it? I was the cursed one, and he was blessed.

From this, I learned that love alone isn't enough.

She found me dwelling in darkness,
So she borrowed some light from the brightest
star in the universe, Sirius,
and confined it within a sunflower,
Left it at my doorstep.

The worn off wounds weren't the gatekeepers,
They were just another threshold for all the
agony to whisper its arrival.

Now, a shard of my soul seeks forgiveness,
A fragment that thought it was within bounds to
show off the crimson traces.

I should have buried them deep,
Maybe this time with a hundred million layers of
love above my soul.

Even if a single layer scatters,
May hell be unleashed unannounced.

Last autumn, the grandest tree in my garden began to shed its leaves and tender blooms.

I couldn't forget the last leaf that refused to fall, eluding even the strongest rainfall.

The droplets from the rain through the leaf felt like a holler, mourning all the other leaves and flowers. Neither time nor the hope she held on to failed to be her ally.

It finally fell to the ground and turned into dust. Mirrored all the people that fell out of my life and never returned.

I wish the roots, and my journey had told us about the spring and new realms first. If we had held on to faith a little longer, unseen flowers and souls would have blossomed.

I'm left with four walls, a window, and a mirror
in my world,
When the sun blesses with light, shadows of
daisies unfurl,
Drawing hope that beyond perception's grasp,
there's beauty untold,
A world that blooms in light, far from the stories
of old.

I'm left with four walls, a window, and a mirror
in my world,
The moon peers through the window, its secrets
swirled,
Unmasking the mysteries I carry inside,
telling me, when days grow dark, I must let my
light collide.

I'm left with four walls, a window, and a mirror
in my world,
The walls spark hope, the window whispers
wisdom swirled,

But the mirror reflects the truth in its stark,
it's not the world that's dark, but me, trapped in
the dark.

My walls yearn for the resonance of your name,
Once a serenade, now imprisoned, it whispers
like a curse.
My pillows contemplate the tears they absorb,
Wondering what once felt heavenly now tastes
like poison.

My pages fret over the poetry I pen these days,
Where words drop like withered petals from the
tallest tree.
The voice, once a serenade,
Heavenly tears once shed,
and words blooming like roses,
now sleeps in the grave woven by the very hand
that birthed him.

When the voice that once bestowed your sacred
song turned silent,
I was the only one to sing your verses, cherished
and true,
yet your deafened ears let my voice fly.

Days later, another flower bloomed,
Knowing the tales behind my broken voice.
Even my mother believed that the fragrance
would mend my wounds forever.
Dawns and dusks have passed, and then I realized
The fragrance's purpose was to ruin what's left
over in my garden.

Now, listen O divine, the malevolent spirit will
be awakened.
Scattered dreams and broken promises will be
answered.
Dear heaven, hold the doors open for hell's
arrival.

#82

Faithful bosoms seek the light, toiling souls yearn for a fruit,
Yet the treacherous label this journey as heaven,
while slumbering spirits are blessed with summer's jewels.

I've spared all my tender shrouds for my beloved's scars,
While my own heart bleeds,
when my treasure turned empty, I was left alone to drown in my misery.

A few days before turning twenty-six, I lay back and ponder,
Is truth the poetic synonym of a lie?

I have been dodging dawns to conceal the shadow that oozes sins from my soul.
What does it take to abandon the malevolent shade that lures euphoric people into hell?
How many more million tears of guilt are enough?

Will this never-ending repentance ever conclude?
Or has the cloak I hide beneath always depicted my true self?

I remember the night I buried the unspoken whispers of my hidden half.
A voice arose from the underworld and inquired, "Why do people bury their past, only to unwrap it later?"

I tremble during the month of September for
what it brings when it ends,
It carries a cascade of memories we spent,
singing along with the whispers of drizzle,
The monsoon has become a melancholic season
now, reminding me of all the roses I brought
you whenever it rained.

I must have thought about you a million times
when a storm tore apart our city a few days ago,
because if I were the city, you were my storm.

I wish I had known you would never come back
to me when you gifted me an umbrella for my
last birthday.

Narrating the bewitching tale of how we fell for each other,
I left a unilateral voyage for all the wounds to heal.
But when the scars unveil how we parted ways at the end,
I wonder if the cuts you left will deepen.

I'm terrified each day as I caught myself loathing all your beloved tunes, shades, and blossoms.
Now the crimson traces aren't yearning for your return, so I named them all after you.

Cause someone in a palest white finery, petals woven all over,
aids me to forsake the life we both dreamt together.

#86

You obliterated the part of my soul that brought
flowers each time we loved a little more,
The kid in me yearned for your mirth every time
you mourned, yet you chose to build a grave
over him.

I have burned hells down at your command, in
return you bestowed me with an adieu text,
Now my knees are trembling to your voices
in my head, I get shakes when I see a flower in
your favorite shade.

But eclipsing the enchanting tale of us with the
violence that followed since we parted ways
is exactly why you couldn't kill the writer in me.

I yearned to raise a farm from the last fruit that's
about to descend from a fading tree.
The storm arrived and showed no mercy the
very next day,
a branch succumbed along with summer's jewel,
extinguishing all the seeds it cradled.

But after the storm's departure, it bestowed
a plant bulb that sprouted into a tree casting
blossom.
Thus, I wished to mourn the demise of my
dream with a flower.
The heavens graced me with ample rain and
sunshine; even a bud blossomed, but the flower
eluded.

I yearned for the fruit to fall, and it did, yet a
farm never flourished.
I aspired for the flower to bloom, it came close,
but never fully unfurled.

When the time calls for my name, I think my
people will end my story saying,
"Almost beautiful, but never was."

I remember reading a story about an alien named
"Ye" nurturing a star some billions of miles
away,
The soul of the star is treasured in the arrays of
flowers that glitter in the shades of white, purple,
and yellow.

One night, she stayed up watching all the
flowers fall. She thought it's time to surrender
her life along with the fading star,
But at dawn, a neighboring galaxy draws near,
restoring both faith and the lost radiance.

She fell asleep among the blooms of bliss,
praying to God never to annihilate the star again,
Only to awaken to a world adorned with dead
flowers.

I halted in my reading and pondered,
"Does the divine save us from death for a
blessing later, or subject us to further suffering?"

She was never the muse of my fantasies,
My cherished sanctuary has forever been my
home,
yet she led me to the river nearby, pointed to the
reflection of us,
and whispered, "home."

I loved receiving journals, and graphite sticks on
my day of birth,
Yet she bestowed upon me a woodland
hammock
and led me on a journey through the wilderness.

When I felt we were falling out of love,
I filled our room with candles, flowers,
and prepared her my favorite meal,
she preferred to rest her weary head upon my
thigh
and reminisce about all the times I made her feel
loved.

She adores the character Amy from *Gone Girl*
For not giving up on her beau Nick,
And I was mad at her for the same reason.

She was never the muse of my fantasies,
But never once did I let a day slip by
Without wishing her to be my forevermore.

#90

It's been a decade since I heard you call my
name,
I remember the twinkle my fingers felt
When I offered you your beloved chocolate
to apologize for the first time,

I remember how your eyes wandered for my
sight
When I showed up as a surprise that one day,
I remember the fragrance of your favorite
shampoo
all over your tresses every Friday,

I remember the taste of our favorite snack
we shared after school,
but I forgot the sound of your tender voice
calling my name, every time I walked past you.

#91

How could I chase butterflies all my life
And rip one's wings when it alights upon my
heart at last?
Was it time that turned me cold,
Or has this been my nature all along?

How dumb of me to get past a simple thought
That we can never go back in time and mend
what's broken.
No matter how many flowers I bloom in the
name of forgiveness
For that one butterfly to thrive,

As long as guilt and regret run through my
veins,
I am but a walking dead man,
Haunted by shadows of my past.

#92

I was reminiscing through all the dawns I
greeted
To endure this sickening journey thus far.
I recall the morning I woke up to meet my best
friends at school,
After a long summer.

Some days I woke up with mild pain all over my
chest,
From staying up late reading our last
conversation.
Amidst it all, one morning stands out vividly,
The day I woke up to my mom's tender tone of
pampering me while I was still asleep.

But today, I woke up all alone on my bed,
Holding on to the regrets from waking up to
live.

The longest night I endured was the time I woke up
from a dreaded nightmare, one I call the echoes
of despair.
A hopeless man was aided by a mystical creature,
assured that she was the answer to all his prayers.

Flowers bloomed and glittered within him as she
held his hand,
And walked him through the alley of all the dark
places he had been through.
And all she ever wanted in return was love,
Not the pearls from the South Sea nor the
flowers from Cape Floral.

He took her to a nearby garden named "lost
love,"
And showed her all the tombstones he had built,
clipped her wings, and buried her.
And I woke up and cursed all the butterflies
That carried my love to its home but never
returned.

#94

You wake up each day with the swallowed past traumas
Resting in your heart just to get through the day,
The creeping pain coursing through your spine
Summons the sleepless nights you've braved.

For endless moonlit hours, you pondered
That one judgment made by someone you held dear to,
and after all the time they took your kindness for granted,
clouding your mind from even smiling at someone new.

Has anyone ever shed their past? Especially when it's all dark and no light?
How do souls move on after letting go?

Then comes the most haunting question,
"Are you okay?" from your dearest friend,
and you go on to utter the same old lie,
"I'm okay" for the millionth time.

Once, beside my mother, I narrated the tale
Of "Cherub's Sole," an ancient bloom so rare.
It graces the air once every seventeen years
And is nurtured by a lonely gardener's blood and
care.

Eyes in the village shone with covetous lust,
Pretending as allies till the day drew near.
The day Cherub's Sole bloomed, the worshippers
turned thieves,
Massacred the gardener's home, and ended his
breath.

The celestial being was torn into a million
pieces,
During the abduction, then marched upon in the
end.
My mother patiently listened to the tale
And uttered, "I wonder if beauty is a curse?"

When life bids me welcome with grim, you taught me to greet it with love.
You were the guardian I sought whenever shadows fell upon my path,
You held my fists and cast a spell of love every time I clenched them to face the world with disgust.

I dreaded all the nightmares twilight brings,
But it was a tender thought of you that brought enchanted rest to my eyes.
Yet, I have been carrying a sense of foreboding
That we may part ways soon.

So, if we do part ways and life turns grim in return,
I promise I will greet it grimly.

Restlessly haunted by memories of you,
Even sleep offers no escape from the nightmares
you bring.

You vowed that your shoulders would be my
refuge forever,
But you let that oath unravel like threads in the
wind.

On the day we parted,
You swore you would leave no signs of your
presence in my life,
and you have honored that vow to this very day.

Yet I remain untroubled
As long as I have a chest filled with leaves and
petals you once touched,
and a playlist alive with songs that breathe your
name.

My only regret is this,
Had I known I'd never see you again,

I would have stayed a bit longer to capture one
last glimpse of your eyes
and hold onto the memory of what I once meant
to you.

Once, I crossed paths with a stage actor in
costume,
His innocent smile stained with blood as he
embodied a long-departed soul.
Unable to resist, I asked, "Why do you paint a
smile with your own blood?"
He answered, "I portray a dead man, burdened
by the guilt of his sins,
Yet upholding the guise of innocence."

As we parted, I journeyed home,
Reflecting on the hearts I had shattered
and the sins I had heaped upon others.
I wondered why this actor seemed so familiar,
Why his eyes mirrored my own.

I halted, turning back to ask his name,
Only to realize I had been staring into a mirror
all along.

Chasing dawn's light was an elusive dream
For someone who emerged from the world of
darkness.
My dawn arrived when it was already too late,
I had breathed in all the shadows my heart could
possibly take in.

Then she appeared, an ethereal woman draped in
endless white fabric,
Adorned with a garden of blooms.
My radiant jewel set herself on fire,
A light that pierced my night, a warmth that
healed even my scars.

Though her flame could not dispel the shadows I
had swallowed,
I promised to carry the light she left
as a memory of her.

In a way, I must have dreamt of sharing three
different lives with you.

In the first, we were neighbors, me at six, you at
four.
I became your first friend, you my first love,
And years later, we married, our tale unfolding
into a happily ever after.

In the second, though we met far too late,
Neither of us had ever loved another.
We married and spent our days longing to have
known each other since childhood.

In the third, we never met.
A mutual friend posted a picture of me with the
words "Gone too soon."
That night, you wandered through my poetry,
Wishing you had found me before anyone else,
knowing you would have loved me.

Now, under the same moon and stars, we met.
You fell for me first, I followed later.

We parted, thinking it was for the best,
Yet both of us wishing this tale had a different
ending.

#101

A storm once ravaged the plants in my garden,
But left a solitary seed at my doorstep, like a
blessing from above.
I sowed it with care, and for days, the sun was
tender and the rain serene.
Hope blossomed within me, though doubt soon
took over,
"Could this delicate sprout ever bear a fruit?" I
wondered

My uncertainty stifled its growth, and it ceased
to flourish.
I abandoned my nurture but held on to my
longing,
Until my neglect, entwined with my yearning,
Brought the plant to its quiet demise.

I sat there for hours, gazing at its lifeless remains,
Reflecting on all the love I've buried so far,
and how they faded in much the same way.

#102

Sometimes I wish to tear open my
chest, pull my heart out, and
scream,
look at the void she left, how many
years does it take to heal?

A hundred million? My heart cries,
"I can never be whole again."

The movies I've watched, the poems I've absorbed, the music I've immersed myself in, and the lyrics I've committed to memory. All led me to believe that love, in its essence, is enough.

Art has this peculiar way of making you believe in miracles, in the idea that love can bind people together and keep them by your side forever.

But the odyssey I've endured has unraveled a harsher truth. It revealed how love can be taken for granted, abandon you in isolation, and erode your faith in humanity.

So, dear fellow hearts, as I pen this poetry of mine, I leave you with this revelation, love alone isn't enough. It is, without question, the most glorified yet overvalued emotion to have ever existed.

#104

In the end, I severed the roots that held your
name in my head,

No echoes of your voice ever rested but tell me,
can a bee ever execrate the lavender's scent?

Dusk is unkind to a heart still mending, with
every fading light, our tale returns.

Hinterland is what I would call our story.
Distant, mysterious and forever unexplored.

Under the same moon where fate once wove us.
I fell. I fought. I withered, and now, I fade into
the night.

From my first poem to this, the journey has led me to find my true self through the loss of the woman I fell for.

The price I paid was heavier than the cosmic leviathan,
And now, for the rest of my life, I must carry it in a heart that once failed to hold even a flower left at my doorstep.

As I unraveled the tales of within, I came to see,
It was I, and I alone, who prayed for a storm
That drowned the flower when all it needed was rain.

At every sacred home, I have been praying to God,
My blessings are hers, and her curses are mine.

And so, I conclude this final poem by saying,

"Had I learned to love another more than myself, this book would have never been written"